The Quality Management Devotional

for Ministry Leaders

by

Joshua T. Fischer, Ph.D.

A Product of

Copyright © 2019 Joshua T. Fischer, Ph.D.

All rights reserved. In accordance with the U.S. Copyright Act of 1976, the scanning, uploading, and electronic sharing of any part of this book without the permission of the publisher constitute unlawful piracy and theft of the author's intellectual property. If you would like to use material from the book (other than for review purposes), prior written permission must be obtained by contacting the publisher at the address below. Thank you for your support of the author's rights.

Progressus Press
13517 E 93rd St N.
Owasso, OK 74055
ProgressusEd.com

Front & Back cover design by Bernell Clifford.

Printed by Ingram.

ISBN: 978-0-578-53995-9 (Paperback)
ISBN: 978-0-578-53996-6 (Electronic Book)

Library of Congress Control Number:2019909804

Printed in the Unites States of America

Forward

I use the YouVersion Bible App nearly every day for my personal devotions. There are thousands of devotionals available on the application. If you haven't downloaded the application to your smart device, I encourage you to do so. Life.Church, the ministry that produced YouVersion, continues to develop resources for the body of Christ completely free. YouVersion is one of those free resources. While an abridged version of this devotional may one day be part of that application, the items that I wished to include in this devotional were more than the current format of YouVersion allows.

The idea for this devotional came from my desire to connect the values of quality management learned through Quality Management Institute's Certified Quality Manager training program with the Christian faith. The values are quite compatible as you'll find.

In this devotional, you'll find coverage of the eight quality manager values as outlined by the Quality Management Institute (QMI). Progressus has gained permission to develop this resource based on the material from QMI's training. However, the views, opinions, and perspectives shared in this devotional are not necessarily the views, opinions, and perspectives of QMI.

As I cover each of the eight values, there will be two focuses: description and action. Within the description section, each will be defined so that you understand the concept. Then, I will show the Biblical perspective on the value in a devotional format. From there, it will be time for you to take action. You will have the opportunity for a self-assessment of your ministry and your personal practice. Additionally, there will be space for you to reflect on what you have learned from our description section and from your self-assessment.

These eight quality management values are broken down into several types. They include vocational values, personal values, Keeping the Promise Culture, and Zero Defects Attitude. Vocational values are focused on work life. Personal values are broader than just work life. Keeping the Promise Culture is a broader concept that requires personal and organizational investment. The Zero Defects Attitude is at the heart of all quality management.

You may find that you complete this in eight hours, eight days, or even eight weeks. Use the timeline that allows you to really reflect well on your own practice.

After completion, there are some additional next steps for you to consider.

You'll also notice that I use "Biblical" instead of "biblical." I understand that the correct grammatical/typographical version of the word is lowercase. However, I have always used "Biblical" as a means of honoring the Word of God.

I hope that you find this devotional meaningful both to your spiritual walk and to your daily practices within your ministry work.

    Joshua

Table of Contents

Forward 1

The What and Why of QM for the Ministry Leader 7

Vocational Certainty 13
    Definition & Discussion 15
    Scriptural Basis & Devotional 17
    Self-Assessment 21
    Reflection 23

Process Quality 25
    Definition & Discussion 27
    Scriptural Basis & Devotional 29
    Self-Assessment 31
    Reflection 33

Administrative Consistency 35
    Definition & Discussion 37
    Scriptural Basis & Devotional 39
    Self-Assessment 43
    Reflection 45

Executive Credibility 47
    Definition & Discussion 49
    Scriptural Basis & Devotional 53
    Self-Assessment 57
    Reflection 59

- Personal Authenticity 61
  - Definition & Discussion 63
  - Scriptural Basis & Devotional 65
  - Self-Assessment 67
  - Reflection 69

- Ethical Dependability 71
  - Definition & Discussion 73
  - Scriptural Basis & Devotional 75
  - Self-Assessment 79
  - Reflection 81

- KTP Culture 83
  - Definition & Discussion 85
  - Scriptural Basis & Devotional 87
  - Self-Assessment 91
  - Reflection 93

- Zero Defects Attitude 95
  - Definition & Discussion 97
  - Scriptural Basis & Devotional 101
  - Self-Assessment 103
  - Reflection 105

- Assessment Review & Reflection 107

- Next Steps 113

THE WHAT AND WHY OF QUALITY MANAGEMENT FOR THE MINISTRY LEADER

Having worked in the field of ministry and served at several churches, I've noticed a recurring problem. Often, the fervency of a local church and its initiatives are held back by the leadership's lack of business and leadership acumen. The pastor and leadership team attempt to lead and manage the operations of the church and struggle to offer sound guidance to the business community church members. However, because they have not had the much-needed education nor the practical business frame of reference, the gap of ineffectiveness widens. This often results in a weakened organizational structure and financial base. For the business owners within the church community, the effects of the lack of business orientation cause feelings of being disenfranchised. This is often demonstrated by organizational conflict and/or progressively pulling away from the church in relevance, attendance, and contributions.

Pastors need the skills to reasonably and competently relate to the business community represented in their congregations and to have the personal and organizational capacity to offer them valuable, Biblically-consistent counseling and training. A spiritually motivated and financially successful business constituency within a congregation inevitably leads to a healthier financial basis for the mission.

Very rarely are courses offered on managing the business side of the church for pastors who are classically trained in a Bible or liberal arts college program. This is problematic in two ways. First, it creates instability in managing the business of the local church; and second, because one of the measures of a healthy church is the spiritual vitality of its members who lead and manage businesses, lack of business understanding leads to the potential for diminishing spiritual vitality in that group. The pastor and leadership team need to be better equipped to minister to this group within the church and counsel them through the circumstances they face as leaders in the business world. However, when a pastor and leadership team do not understand how to effectively operate the business of the church and/or to effectively help and encourage its business community members, a series of diminishing returns is created for both the church and its members.

Churches that are stable and growing have been successful in developing and maintaining these operational leadership elements. At a time when we see a rise in the post-Christian culture (Barna, 2015), a lack of understanding and applying operational best practices means the difference between a church accomplishing its mission and reaching the local community in sustainable ways or one that becomes another example of the failure of the church.

This is where quality management (or QM) is key. "Quality management is an educational technology with systems, methods, and language" that "helps us reach our business and organizational goals" (Kennedy, n.d.). Within the non-profit organization, QM allows the organization to develop extra reserves that will assist in accomplishing new aspects of the organizational mission, carry the organization during times of lower income, and help the leadership care well for both those serving as employees within the ministry and those the ministry serves.

References

Barna Group. (2015). *2015 sees sharp rise in post-Christian population.* Retrieved March 8, 2019 from https://www.barna.com/research/2015-sees-sharp-rise-in-post-christian-population/

Kennedy, L. (n.d.). *QM and profitability.* [Online video]. Available from http://www.qualitymanagementinstitute.com

VOCATIONAL CERTAINTY

Vocational Certainty
Definition & Discussion

In quality management terms, vocational certainty is a vocational value regarding your work life. Vocationally certain individuals have the necessary training and education, talents, skill sets, and the emotional maturity to accomplish their work. They have the willingness to perform their work with excellence. The vocationally certain continue to develop their skills so that they can manage the processes for which they are responsible.

Within the church or other ministry, we can all probably think of individuals who have not been vocationally certain . . . and don't just look at the youth pastor. Employees and ministerial staff at all levels have entered roles being under-prepared for the work ahead of them, lacking talent to lead people, prepare sermons, manage budgets, etc. They enter their work for the ministry emotionally unstable and unwilling to be ready to work with excellence.

I was a member of a large church where the associate pastor was vocationally uncertain. When he preached, we all groaned because he did nothing to connect with the congregation. It wasn't that he was just a poor preacher. His poor preaching became an indicator and demonstration of his work as a minister. It got so bad that we didn't want to attend when he was preaching. It finally came to a head when one Sunday, we arrived at church and the head pastor announced that the associate pastor was no longer with us. He explained to the church that the associate pastor had been encouraged to consider different roles when new opportunities arose. However, he would simply not do anything different in his practice at the current church nor would he take another role. Finally, the head pastor gave him a month to find a role that would be better suited for him elsewhere. Instead of taking the opportunity and being emotionally mature, he left overnight.

This lack of vocational certainty is clear to parishioners, constituents, and those in the community when they come in contact with an individual who doesn't have it. The missing ingredient in their practice is striking when results are affected by this lack.

Vocational Certainty
Scriptural Basis & Devotional

But the wisdom that comes from heaven is first of all pure; then peace-loving, considerate, submissive, full of mercy and good fruit, impartial and sincere.

James 3:17 (NIV)

The vocation we choose is central to the fulfillment of our human desires for life, family, personal achievement, and spiritual growth. So, it follows that nothing could be more relevant to the development of the vision for our life and profession than to have a clear understanding of our vocational strengths and weaknesses. We can remedy some weaknesses by acquiring knowledge, skills, etc. On the other hand, other weaknesses might be clear indicators that we are likely more suited for profession "B" than profession "A." Conversely, strengths can be milestones that help define a reliable route toward fulfilling our hopes and dreams.

To be sure that we are pursuing the right agenda, we should judge the validity of our vision through the lens of some important questions.

Do I have a sense of intellectual integrity about this idea? Are the thoughts and motives that are energizing me pure before God? Are my plans really clear? Do my gifts and talents naturally support what I am considering?

Do I have a clear moral conscience about this plan? Am I at peace and are the steps I have taken producing peace in me? Or, do I really feel uneasy, but have pushed on because I want or need something more than I should?

Am I being faithful to the task? Are my actions reasonable when I take steps to fulfill my objective or do I find myself becoming unreasonably aggressive? Am I forcing things to happen as opposed to gently and carefully stewarding my responsibilities?

Am I making a reasonable judgment? Is this plan reasonable? Does it pass the test of common sense or am I rationalizing facts and events? When I consider giving up, do I feel peaceful and free, and exhibit the "fruit" of God's Spirit, or do I feel angry and desperate? Is there any wavering within me, or hypocrisy in what I am considering? Am I really speaking truth to myself or is there conflict in my heart?

These are the difficult questions that must be asked. If they are not asked and answered, we could find ourselves making very bad decisions; and, discover too late that our vision is critically flawed.

Vocational Certainty
Self-Assessment

Using the scoring scale, rate each area of the question. At the end of the Assessment, tally the score by letter (i.e. tally the totals for A, B, and C, separately).

On a scale of 1 to 5, where 1 is Never, 2 is Hardly Ever, 3 is Some of the Time, 4 is Most of the Time, and 5 is All of the Time,

1) How often is each group equipped to do the work they are assigned (through skills, education, talents, gifts):
    A. Each of the leaders in the organization?
    B. Each of the team members in your area?
    C. You?
2) How often does each group act emotionally mature:
    A. Each of the leaders in the organization?
    B. Each of the team members in your area?
    C. You?
3) How often does each group perform with excellence:
    A. Each of the leaders in the organization?

B. Each of the team members in your area?

   C. You?

4) How often does each group continue to develop the skills needed to manage processes within their responsibility areas:

   A. Each of the leaders in the organization?

   B. Each of the team members in your area?

   C. You?

	Place your response for each question in the appropriate cell. Total the columns in the "T" row at the bottom.		
	Total of A — Leaders in the Organization	Total of B — Team Members in your Area	Total of C — You
1			
2			
3			
4			
T			

Vocational Certainty
Reflection

PROCESS QUALITY

Process Quality
Definition & Discussion

Process quality is another of the vocational values within quality management. Developing the plans and budgeting the resources needed to accomplish the plan are both vital to develop products and/or services that are beneficial and consistent for the customer or constituent. That's process quality. Without it, results are not replicable and quality is not consistent.

A quality leader must always work to determine the facts of the situation. Process quality is about collecting those facts through effective planning and budgeting that is rational and unbiased in light of the facts. For the quality leader, it's not about being right; it is about finding the right solution by submitting biases to a process.

As a practical application of process quality in ministry, imagine starting a building project without a plan or budget. Constituents, parishioners, and community members would come to you asking for details about how much it would cost, what the new building's purpose would be, how long it would take to build, etc. Without going through the steps to develop the plans and budgets, you would not have the answers and it would never be completed.

Maintaining good process quality forces you (and your team) to understand what needs to happen for the outcome (product, service, building) to be a good one.

As another example, imagine you wanted to add a new outreach to your ministry. You would want to fully describe the purpose of the outreach, research how it should be done correctly, figure out all the costs involved to develop and implement the new outreach, and then decide on how you will implement. Only then would the outreach be much more likely to succeed and be effective. This gives you, the designer, the information you need to more fully develop the quality outreach you desire to implement.

It is important to note that process quality is not limited to big-ticket items. Process quality applies to the smallest level work that you hope to have ongoing within your organization. Even a mini-version of process quality should become a part of daily decisions. As you become more and more used to putting yourself through the steps of ensuring process quality, you will more naturally focus on making sure you cover all your bases. As you will see in the devotional, being diligent in even the smallest of processes keeps huge mistakes from happening.

Process Quality
Scriptural Basis & Devotional

> *Where there is no vision [no revelation of God and His word], the people are unrestrained; But happy and blessed is he who keeps the law [of God].*
> Proverbs 29:18 (AMP)

It's often stated that "Leaders must have a 'big' vision" to motivate their followers to action: something that requires the complete unity of the team, a riveting focus on the objectives, and what the participants believe is a vision of, for, and from God. This may sound really attractive to someone who's never actually had to lead people on what General George Patton once called "a desperate mission." But once you've had to struggle through the details of project management, the high-minded words which initially described your vision sound much less heroic and romantic, even when you're successful.

What's more difficult is to find reality after a defeat, especially when you were so sure it was a "God-thing." It's usually after one of these sobering moments that a maturing leader realizes that he or she will happily trade "big, or exciting, or transformative" or the other words that we'd used to draw people to our vision, for words like "real, reliable, accurate, and achievable."

Sometimes we can find ourselves rushing past the facts to achieve an outcome. In a world of "agile and lean" concepts, the due diligence, rigor, and systems thinking that create reliable processes to support our vision can be unwisely ignored. When that happens, we often find a very sobering and sometimes terrifying awakening that awaits our arrival at the limits of our abilities.

The "law of God" is more than moral, ethical, and spiritual dogma. It's full of values, principles, and methodologies that will guide those who "keep" or "follow" it to discover a bad idea disguised as a good one. This is the kind of idea that comes to mind as a flash of exciting vision but proves to be less than doable. Alternatively, we can discover the principle that facts provide a basis for wisdom and adjustments to help us avoid failure and turn a potentially sad learning experience into a success.

Process Quality Self-Assessment

Using the scoring scale, rate each area of the question. At the end of the Assessment, tally the score by letter (i.e. tally the totals for A, for B, and C, separately).

On a scale of 1 to 5, where 1 is Never, 2 is Hardly Ever, 3 is Some of the Time, 4 is Most of the Time, and 5 is All of the Time,

1) How often are strategic plans developed and shared to accomplish organizational level goals by:
    A. Each of the leaders in the organization?
    B. Each of the team members in your area?
    C. You?
2) How often are strategic plans developed and shared to accomplish departmental or project goals or general work processes by:
    A. Each of the leaders in the organization?
    B. Each of the team members in your area?
    C. You?
3) How often are budgets developed and actually used for the organization at large by:
    A. Each of the leaders in the organization?

      B. Each of the team members in your area?
      C. You?
4) How often are budgets developed and actually used for individual projects by:
      A. Each of the leaders in the organization?
      B. Each of the team members in your area?
      C. You?

	Place your response for each question in the appropriate cell. Total the columns in the "T" row at the bottom.		
	Total of A — Leaders in the Organization	Total of B — Team Members in your Area	Total of C — You
1			
2			
3			
4			
T			

Process Quality Reflection

ADMINISTRATIVE CONSISTENCY

Administrative Consistency
Definition & Discussion

A third vocational value in quality management is administrative consistency. Administrative consistency is a measure of attention to the details of your work, whether it is the details of tasks, of protocols and procedures, of paperwork, or of constituent requirements. A quality leader will pay attention to those details to make sure the numbers are correct and the lists are complete and finished.

In a ministry, listening to our constituents and/or parishioners is vital as the ministry is so dependent on the support of those groups. When leaders forge on ahead without proper research and without listening to their members, they will likely fail to get the support they need and not balance their own bias about a topic.

For many churches, the rise in popularity of non-traditional service times is a point of interest. Some churches have been highly successful with Saturday services and even Friday and Monday services. For some, online services have been successful. However, church leaders must properly review details about providing those services and listen to the demands of constituents before jumping into offering them. The popularity of those services elsewhere cannot sustain those services for every church.

In my community, a large church offers two services on Saturday, six services on Sunday, and one service on Monday on a regular basis. They also offer 80+ online services throughout the week. They are highly impactful and reach a large portion of the community both at the local campus and online, and are one of the largest churches in the world.

Several years ago, another local church wanted to attempt Saturday evening services to capitalize on what seemed to be demand. Unfortunately, after attempting the service for some time, it was still not well attended. Additionally, it was burning the staff out who were all required to be at a service attended by only a few parishioners. They finally shelved the idea to the great relief of the staff.

The difference in the two examples is that the first church made their decisions by giving attention to the details (internally, externally, listening to internal and external constituents, and adjusting based on those details) and the other did not.

Administrative Consistency
Scriptural Basis & Devotional

It is the glory of God to conceal a matter; to search out a matter is the glory of kings.
Proverbs 25:2 (NIV)

It's possible to dread and either consciously or unconsciously resist completing the tasks that will bring clarity to a project and determine your path to success or failure. And if you hate administrative tasks, it's a good indicator that you might also be resisting other forms of personal or professional "discipline" that are essential to your success. Someone once said, "Having administrative duties to complete is often an indicator of prosperity." In other words, you wouldn't have certain tasks to complete if your vision (or work-life) was failing. When your vision is sitting dead in the water without wind in your sails, you might long for those nasty administrative duties. The things that you've wrongly thought kept you entangled and away from the "creative" part of your work might just be the "mess in the cow's stall" that indicates something good ... like productivity.

That's often the way it is with research and keeping lists of requirements that will define both the path and processes you need to be successful. Hebrews 12 tells us that

> *All discipline for the moment seems not to be joyful, but sorrowful; yet to those who have been trained by it, afterwards it yields the peaceful fruit of righteousness*
> Heb 12:11 (NIV)

It often feels like God conceals a matter so we can endure the discipline required to seek out the matter and then enjoy the "peaceful fruit of righteousness" we gain by properly "enduring." Endurance is not the ability to survive and be robot-like in obedience through difficulties; it's an attribute of righteousness that's attained through practice, repetitions, re-enforcements, and the wisdom it produces.

To "search out a matter" has greater importance than just finding the right facts and getting the logistical or organizational attributes of your vision properly aligned. Of course, these are legitimate reasons to apply ourselves to research. But to follow the Biblical principles faithfully and with a believing heart, yields much greater dividends; not the least of which is a greater intimacy with God.

If we are organizational leaders or just individuals who are values-based and facts-driven, we require the emotional sobriety and rational stability to honestly evaluate our choices of path, methods, available resources, and, most importantly, what we believe is compatible with our faith.

In other words, the pursuit of reliable facts and perceptions through research together with the objective analysis of the facts and their impact on our faith, is essential.

Administrative Consistency Self-Assessment

Using the scoring scale, rate each area of the question. At the end of the Assessment, tally the score by letter (i.e. tally the totals for A, for B, and C, separately).

On a scale of 1 to 5, where 1 is Never, 2 is Hardly Ever, 3 is Some of the Time, 4 is Most of the Time, and 5 is All of the Time,

1) How often is attention given to the details of the work you do by
    A. Each of the leaders in the organization?
    B. Each of the team members in your area?
    C. You?
2) How often is care demonstrated for customer needs and job requirements from the customer by
    A. Each of the leaders in the organization?
    B. Each of the team members in your area?
    C. You?
3) How often is paperwork (reports, order forms, etc.) accurate from
    A. Each of the leaders in the organization?

B. Each of the team members in your area?
C. You?
4) How often are the proper protocols and procedures used by
   A. Each of the leaders in the organization?
   B. Each of the team members in your area?
   C. You?

	Place your response for each question in the appropriate cell. Total the columns in the "T" row at the bottom.		
	Total of A — Leaders in the Organization	Total of B — Team Members in your Area	Total of C — You
1			
2			
3			
4			
T			

Administrative Consistency
Reflection

EXECUTIVE CREDIBILITY

Executive Credibility
Definition & Discussion

The final vocational value of quality management is executive credibility, which is a measure of skill and sincerity with people. As a quality leader, you must regularly deal with people well in order to accomplish the work to which you've been called. While many ministry leaders are good at interacting with people in some facet, there is often a missing component or two in their practice such as being engaging in the pulpit but struggling one-on-one. A larger issue, however, usually relates to the management of human resources within the ministry.

To have executive credibility, you must commit yourself to practices that help you *be* credible. A leader with executive credibility works to have reasonable discussions with those inside and outside his or her organization. Listening to and maintaining concern for the other speaker in the conversation demonstrates this facet of the credible leader. When interacting with people, making sure you are not manipulating, pushing, or pressuring them to do what you want done, but presenting them with the facts of the situation and working with them to accomplish what needs to be done, effectively makes you a more credible leader.

You've probably heard the slogan that "Quality is Job 1." Getting the job done right *is* a great indicator of executive credibility for the leader. If a leader continually fails to get the job done right, his/her reputation will continue to sink because credibility is lacking based on that track record of failure.

A leader who is naturally sincere from the heart is one with executive credibility. You've probably also heard the adage that "people don't care how much you know until they know how much you care." Sincerity will connect you to people better than the facts and figures you retain in your head.

Quality leaders improve executive credibility by continually developing themselves and their skills. By learning how to do things better, people around you begin to notice your improved abilities. I've watched as pastors and other leaders go through education and training. When they use that training to grow in their roles, and not just "put on airs" because they've advanced their degree, it's amazing how people react to their new understanding. The useful, personal development is like a people magnet for the leader.

Clear and competent communication is vital for the quality leader. When communication is plagued with poor grammar, an unclear message, poor timing, or ineffective delivery, it reflects so strongly on the credibility of the leader and/or organization.

Each of these demonstrates a leader's skill and sincerity with people around them, whether from the pulpit, talking to individuals, or leading the human resources within the ministry. Without the focus on each of these areas, the ministry leader loses executive credibility.

Executive Credibility
Scriptural Basis & Devotional

Leaders with Executive Credibility can accurately discern risks and rewards, choose reliable solutions, and clearly explain their plans to their constituents. Executive Credibility is a measure of our sincerity and skill with people. Sincerity comes naturally from the heart. You either have it or you don't. But skills can be sharpened and improved. By adding QM values and methods to your routines, people will gain confidence in your leadership, especially when you take time to listen to them and give them clear, competent answers.

When people know from personal experience that we are who we say we are and that we will be just and fair in the conduct of our business, they are more likely to cooperate with us. But if a person's integrity or wisdom is in doubt, people will express their feelings about his or her leadership in ways that are detrimental to the mission. To grow in influence, we must demonstrate emotional maturity as well as competence because when a person is perceived to be "kind, honest and fair, his kingdom stands secure" (Proverbs 20:28 [TLB]).

In Isaiah 42: 1-4 (NIV) the writer speaks prophetically of Jesus:

> *Here is my servant, whom I uphold, my chosen one in whom I delight; I will put my Spirit on Him and He will bring justice to the nations, He will not shout or cry out, or raise His voice in the streets. A bruised reed He will not break, and a smoldering wick He will not snuff out. In faithfulness He will bring forth justice; He will not falter or be discouraged until He establishes justice on the earth.*

Leaders who are growing in these attributes will invoke the greatest confidence in the constituency that forms around them. They will function under the grace of the Spirit of God, not shouting, crying out, or raising their voices. They will not be eager to break off or snuff out the value of another person's contribution. And they will not falter or become discouraged until they establish justice where they lead. The implications here go far beyond the administration of work or the judgments that are required to establish equity. This scripture describes an individual who understands how to be an example of justice.

The Hebrew word translated as "justice" is most commonly translated as just or justice, such as in 1 Chronicles 18:14 (NIV):

David reigned over all of Israel, doing what was just and right for all his people.

However, it is also translated as "dimensions, specifications, standards, regulations, ordinances, practices, precepts, requirements, the prescribed way, and the proper time and procedure." It tells us that to faithfully bring forth justice, we must demonstrate the right way to do things in both word and deed.

Executive Credibility
Self-Assessment

Using the scoring scale, rate each area of the question. At the end of the Assessment, tally the score by letter (i.e. tally the totals for A, for B, and C, separately).

On a scale of 1 to 5, where 1 is Never, 2 is Hardly Ever, 3 is Some of the Time, 4 is Most of the Time, and 5 is All of the Time,

1) How often is sincerity towards people demonstrated by
    A. Each of the leaders in the organization?
    B. Each of the team members in your area?
    C. You?
2) How often are discussions logical and reasonable by
    A. Each of the leaders in the organization?
    B. Each of the team members in your area?
    C. You?
3) How often is interaction free of manipulation, pressuring, or pushing by
    A. Each of the leaders in the organization?

       B. Each of the team members in your area?
       C. You?
4) How often is communication clear and competent by
       A. Each of the leaders in the organization?
       B. Each of the team members in your area?
       C. You?

	Place your response for each question in the appropriate cell. Total the columns in the "T" row at the bottom.		
	Total of A — Leaders in the Organization	Total of B — Team Members in your Area	Total of C — You
1			
2			
3			
4			
T			

Executive Credibility Reflection

PERSONAL AUTHENTICITY

Personal Authenticity
Definition & Discussion

With the value of personal authenticity, we move into the personal values of the quality manager. This aspect is fairly understandable in the wording. To be authentic is to be credible and real; based on facts; not false, phony, or fraudulent.

When leaders are personally authentic, they are who they say they are. They are transparent in their dealings with customers, coworkers, and everyone in their lives.

We've probably all experienced people who lack personal authenticity. They come off as snake-oil salesmen. They are shady and shifty. You always expect they have some trick up their sleeve.

The auto industry is rife with examples of those who lack personal authenticity from used car salespeople to mechanics who try to fool the unknowing into purchasing repairs they don't need. When you find one who is credible and real, you will gladly pay for the quality you receive.

Those in ministry obviously should reflect personal authenticity. Sadly, here, too, we see examples of the phony where everything is about the buck that can be made from adherents' donations.

I once worked with a ministry where the leader lost his personal authenticity. He became so focused on money, that the offertory "sermon" was longer than the main sermon. Letters for support spoke of the leader needing funds for a new private jet because he "needed to get home to [his] children." For those in the know, the children of this leader were both graduated from high school and in college . . . despite the inference in the support letter that they were small children.

When the message moves beyond what is real and credible, not based on fact, the message of the gospel is tarnished.

Personal Authenticity
Scriptural Basis & Devotional

The aim of our charge is love that issues from a pure heart and a good conscience and a sincere faith.
I Timothy 1:5 (ESV)

Personal Authenticity is a measure of our resolve to live a consistent life. It is an indicator of the sensitivity of our conscience and how obediently we respond to the conviction of the Holy Spirit. True accountability begins in the recesses of the heart, where our hidden will and desires are tested by our knowledge of the will of God. The choices we make to discipline our souls, bring consistency to our words and deeds, and obey the Lord, are the ultimate proof of our credibility.

One of the dictionary definitions of faith is fidelity (or faithfulness) to one's promises; something that is believed with strong conviction as a system of religious beliefs. A classical Greek definition of faith is to be "morally persuaded of the truth." The success we experience as leaders and ethical change-agents will greatly depend on how morally persuaded we are about the need for change and then how faithfully we model the values and principles of our management doctrine. But the most emotionally challenging test for us as leaders is to live consistently with those things we are morally persuaded are true and right, even if the decisions we make affect people's motivations or livelihood in a negative way.

As leaders, we are obligated to empower the promises we make by keeping the fire of the Zero Defects heart attitude (discussed later) burning brightly. An essential element for "fanning the flame" is getting it right on the decisions we make. But the more important question is, "How can we know our information is reliable?" Simply put, reliable methods produce reliable results.

Personal Authenticity is at the heart of every leader's credibility, whether it's in a spiritual role that's intended to model his or her faith, in a job description based on business or science competencies, or, as is more likely, a real-world demand for both. The faith we need to make a personal decision spiritually or as a workplace leader springs from the same source of values and facts that carry us to the place of being morally persuaded that what we've decided is "true and right." This is consistent with the dictionary definition of "wisdom" which is "knowledge of what is true and right coupled with good judgment."

Personal Authenticity
Self-Assessment

Using the scoring scale, rate each area of the question. At the end of the Assessment, tally the score by letter (i.e. tally the totals for A, for B, and C, separately).

On a scale of 1 to 5, where 1 is Never, 2 is Hardly Ever, 3 is Some of the Time, 4 is Most of the Time, and 5 is All of the Time,

1) How often is authenticity demonstrated by
    A. Each of the leaders in the organization?
    B. Each of the team members in your area?
    C. You?
2) How often is integrity demonstrated by
    A. Each of the leaders in the organization?
    B. Each of the team members in your area?
    C. You?
3) How often are decisions reliable and fact-based as made by
    A. Each of the leaders in the organization?
    B. Each of the team members in your area?
    C. You?

4) How often is transparency demonstrated by
   A. Each of the leaders in the organization?
   B. Each of the team members in your area?
   C. You?

	Place your response for each question in the appropriate cell. Total the columns in the "T" row at the bottom.		
	Total of A — Leaders in the Organization	Total of B — Team Members in your Area	Total of C — You
1			
2			
3			
4			
T			

Personal Authenticity Reflection

ETHICAL DEPENDABILITY

Ethical Dependability
Definition & Discussion

Ethics seems a common conversation in our culture today. Not that it is high but that it is low. We see the examples of poor ethics in companies like Enron, Equifax, Wells Fargo, and many others. It has created a general distrust of businesses worldwide, including non-profit organizations and churches.

Ethical dependability, however, is a key piece of the quality manager's practice. The ethically dependable manager is known for being trustworthy in practical matters and reliable in his or her dealings with financial and people matters.

You might expect the ethics of a church or ministry to be Biblically centered, and, therefore, free of ethical problems. However, that is not the case. From smaller issues where the head pastor has removed the power of the board through cronyism or outright dissolution, to cases of embezzlement where leaders used the ministry as their personal slush fund, ethical dependability has taken a beating in ministries and churches.

In church and ministry settings, idolatry and fear-based fellowship can be, ironically, very real issues.

"Follow me as I follow Jesus" may be the mentality that those lacking in ethical dependability espouse to their congregations/constituents all the while living a distorted and sinful life.

Quality managers are known for being honest and direct in their dealings. There aren't shades of gray when dealing with ethically dependable individuals.

For organizations desiring to test ethical dependability of their team members, the key is to start out with limited amounts of money and limited amounts of authority. In starting with small amounts, it allows the organization to know whether they can be faithful with the small amounts before trying them out on larger ones. The individual then develops a proven track record. This starts from the top, with a new ministry leader reporting to the board as he or she is tested in small matters first.

Ethical Dependability
Scriptural Basis & Devotional

Even a child makes himself known by his acts, by whether his conduct is pure and upright.
Proverbs 20:11 (ESV)

Ethical Dependability is a measure of our trustworthiness in practical matters. It's an indicator of the confidence that others have in us that we will be honest, fair, and faithful. These qualities are critical in a leader if people are going to rely on him or her to make good decisions. They are essential not only in our personal life and family, but also to the success of any career or ministry we will have. If you want to be trusted, you should strive to develop reliable ethics and good judgment.

Who among us has not said, "I would like to do that all over again with what I now know." When we look back at how things "could have been," we can see how some of the most important decisions we have made were affected by our character. Greed, passion, or the personal need for power may have caused us to say "yes" to a risky idea when a more secure, disciplined person would have declined. Or careful and prudent analysis could have helped us properly evaluate the ethics of a business relationship that would later prove to be unsavory.

There might also have been times when the fear of failure or our questionable judgment neutralized us and left us unable to take advantage of reasonable opportunities when they occurred. As we gain experience in life, we can begin to figure out what did or did not work for us in different situations and decide how things can be done better in the future. When these reflective times reveal problems with our values and strategies, they become opportunities "for acquiring a disciplined and prudent life" and "doing what is right and just and fair" (Proverbs 1:3).

A person's value system operates like a program in a computer. It is a complex set of interrelated ideas, learned experiences, and personal theories through which information is processed, analyzed, and output as actions to be taken. It includes all the values and strategies we have collected over our lifetime along with the various priorities we have assigned them. When we have to make a decision, this program with all its preset ideas and concepts (good and bad, accurate and inaccurate) begins to converge on the problem in an effort to come to a conclusion about the correct action to take and the strength with which it should be executed. Changing the viewpoint of just one item in our program to a more reliable perspective can have enormously positive effects.

People need a consistent role model of what is being requested before they will trust someone and respond to them properly. Without it, people will either refuse to follow their leader or will cooperate for the wrong reasons, such as fear, idolatry, or intimidation. The influence that character has on good judgment and behavior cannot be minimized. It is the real issue behind many of the failures that occur at home and at work. In fact, reliable character is a person's most important asset. For the ministry leader, reliable character is, perhaps, even more important than for the average person because the trust level is so implicit for success of ministry.

We begin to shape our character early in life as we learn the principles that will become the foundation for our values and strategies. They include the significance of truth, what is just and fair, the difference between responsible and irresponsible actions, respect for the rights and property of others, the need for compassion and faithfulness in relationships, and how to exercise moral restraint. Everything else we learn or do is affected by these fundamentals.

Ethical Dependability Self-Assessment

Using the scoring scale, rate each area of the question. At the end of the Assessment, tally the score by letter (i.e. tally the totals for A, for B, and C, separately).

On a scale of 1 to 5, where 1 is Never, 2 is Hardly Ever, 3 is Some of the Time, 4 is Most of the Time, and 5 is All of the Time,

1) How often is a high ethical standard demonstrated by
    A. Each of the leaders in the organization?
    B. Each of the team members in your area?
    C. You?
2) How often is reliability with money demonstrated by
    A. Each of the leaders in the organization?
    B. Each of the team members in your area?
    C. You?
3) How often is honesty and directness demonstrated by
    A. Each of the leaders in the organization?

B. Each of the team members in your area?
   C. You?

4) How often is trustworthiness demonstrated by
   A. Each of the leaders in the organization?
   B. Each of the team members in your area?
   C. You?

	Place your response for each question in the appropriate cell. Total the columns in the "T" row at the bottom.		
	Total of A — Leaders in the Organization	Total of B — Team Members in your Area	Total of C — You
1			
2			
3			
4			
T			

Ethical Dependability
Reflection

KTP CULTURE

KTP Culture
Definition & Discussion

KTP stands for Keeping the Promise and refers to the type of mindset required in quality management. As quality managers, we must always work to keep the promises we make to coworkers, clients, constituents, and parishioners. To extend that, we as leaders need to make our culture embrace this mindset.

At the foundation of a KTP Culture is mutual respect, accountability, and professionalism. When leaders show mutual respect for each other, they are helping to promote the accomplishment of the organization. Even when disagreements arise, mutual respect keeps them from turning into wars that tear away at the organization.

Accountability may be a dirty word to some because it seems to limit freedom. However, when we set boundaries and remain accountable both to the mutually-agreed-upon boundaries and to each other, we get a freedom that allows us to run without always worrying about risk of doing wrong. The child who is accountable to his parents by staying in the yard knows he's free of getting hit by a car by playing in the street.

When a standard of professionalism is set in the culture, there is a known quantity by which to measure. A friend of mine owns his own insurance agency and has a "no jeans" policy except for specific times. When pressed on the policy by some, he reminds them that this is a standard of professionalism that they keep to honor customers. In a previous position I held, married individuals did not ride with members of the opposite sex alone. That standard of professionalism honored the sanctity of marriage and protected the individual.

The KTP culture, founded on these qualities, needs to be stated in your organizational values and empowered by the actions of the leader's practice. Without willingness to state the values and actually practice them, the culture cannot be established.

One of my favorite quotes about culture is attributed to Peter Drucker and Mark Fields (and slightly modified by Bill Aulet). Setting the culture is vital and KTP is a strong way to do it.

> *Culture eats strategy for breakfast, technology for lunch, and products for dinner, and soon thereafter everything else too.*

KTP Culture
Scriptural Basis & Devotional

Each of us will experience tyranny at some time in our life. Because Proverbs 25:26 tells us that a person who yields to tyranny is like a "muddied spring or a polluted well," it's very important to know what to do, especially at work, while we wait upon the deliverance of the Lord. Here are some suggestions:

1) Don't be afraid. "The fear of man brings a snare, but he who trusts in the Lord will be exalted" (Proverbs 29:25 [NAS]). Jesus said,

> *I tell you friends, do not be afraid of those who can kill the body and after that can do no more. But I will show you whom you should fear. Fear him who, after the killing of the body, has power to throw you into hell. Yes, I tell you fear him. Are not five sparrows sold for two pennies? Yet not one of them is forgotten by God. Indeed, the very hairs of your head are numbered. Don't be afraid; you are worth more than many sparrows.*
>
> Luke 12:5-7 (NIV)

2) Unless you are asked to do something illegal or immoral, obey your earthly masters in everything. Keep doing your job, and do it, not only when their

eye is on you and to win favor, but with sincerity of heart and reverence for the Lord.

> *Whatever you do, work at it with all your heart, as working for the Lord, not for human masters, since you know that you will receive an inheritance from the Lord as a reward. It is the Lord Christ you are serving.*
>
> Colossians 3:22-24 (NIV)

3) Be prepared to hold your superiors accountable without trying to exercise authority or influence you do not have. All that is required is that you speak the truth humbly. Remember,

> *God has not given us the spirit of timidity, but of power, love and discipline [or sound judgment].*
> 2 Timothy 1:7 (NAS)

4) Be prepared to make an investment of suffering. Tyrants and the people around them do not like being told they are wrong. Proverbs 29:16 (TLB) says,

> *When rulers are wicked, their people are too; but good men will live to see the tyrant's downfall.*

Just remember,

> *Who is there to harm you if you prove zealous for what is good? But even if you should suffer for the sake of righteousness, you are blessed. Do not fear their intimidation, and do not be troubled, but sanctify Christ as Lord in your heart, always being able to give an account for the hope that is in you, yet with gentleness and reverence. Keep a good conscience so that in the thing in which you are slandered, those who revile your good behavior in Christ may be put to shame. For it is better, if God should will it so, that you suffer for doing what is right rather than for doing what is wrong.*
> 1 Peter 3: 13-17 (NAS)

Effective leaders often describe how they take time to look honestly into their own hearts and minds and answer this simple two-part question: How much fear and insecurity do I actually have about the work I do; and how can people in my workspace positively or negatively affect the outcomes of my efforts? Healthy introspection can lead to important discoveries about who we are and why we say and do the things we say and do. And what usually follows is opportunity for improvement. Personal and professional success is related to what we can do to change—to learn and grow—so our performance measures continue to push the envelope of excellence. We can improve through self-analysis and introspection, through feedback from our working environment, or through a combination of both. But one thing is certain, managers and leaders are either improving to build a better tomorrow or slowly deteriorating in a false equilibrium of "activity disguised as achievement."

KTP Culture
Self-Assessment

Using the scoring scale, rate each area of the question. At the end of the Assessment, tally the score by letter (i.e. tally the totals for A, for B, and C, separately).

On a scale of 1 to 5, where 1 is Never, 2 is Hardly Ever, 3 is Some of the Time, 4 is Most of the Time, and 5 is All of the Time,

1) How often is a sense of mutual respect demonstrated by
    A. Each of the leaders in the organization?
    B. Each of the team members in your area?
    C. You?
2) How often is accountability to others demonstrated by
    A. Each of the leaders in the organization?
    B. Each of the team members in your area?
    C. You?
3) How often is a standard of professionalism demonstrated by
    A. Each of the leaders in the organization?

B. Each of the team members in your area?
   C. You?

4) How often is value of the work of the organization connected to fulfilling constituent requirements and needs demonstrated by
   A. Each of the leaders in the organization?
   B. Each of the team members in your area?
   C. You?

	Place your response for each question in the appropriate cell. Total the columns in the "T" row at the bottom.		
	Total of A	Total of B	Total of C
	Leaders in the Organization	Team Members in your Area	You
1			
2			
3			
4			
T			

KTP Culture
Reflection

ZERO DEFECTS
ATTITUDE

Zero Defects Attitude
Definition & Discussion

Just what is this "Zero Defects Attitude" anyway? Some of you will think that defects only apply to products. Others might hear "zero defects" and think no mistakes are allowed. Neither is the case. The Zero Defects Attitude is not about having <u>no</u> mistakes or errors in practices, procedures, services, and products of the individual and/or organization.

ZDA is a heart attitude that the quality manager holds. It's a sense of pride in the workmanship he or she delivers. Rather than focusing on perfection, which is impossible given our fallen nature, the focus of ZDA is never allowing an error or mistake to be "acceptable." ZDA, in practice, inherently works to keep the promise to others. An attitude that works to remove defects from products and services always has the promise made as its focus.

You may think this is a semantic argument between allowing some mistakes and not accepting them as "okay." Some strands of quality management actually allow for a statistical degree of error in their process, products, and services because they know mistakes will be made. Unfortunately, that method simply sanctions the incompetence that leads to errors and mistakes rather than preventing them.

As an example, how many flies are acceptable in the burger you intend to eat? Unless you're into eating bugs, your answer is probably "zero." So, to keep the promise to the client, the quality manager is not going to accept even one fly in the burger as okay. If one is found, the quality manager will make it right for the customer. In doing so, the quality manager continually works to keep errors and mistakes out of the practice. That silly example is fairly benign, albeit gross (if you're not into eating bugs).

However, let's take the principle further. What if a tire company has an acceptable level of error in the production of its tires? What happens if that error in the production of the tires happens at 75 miles per hour on the highway, in traffic, with small children? What if the defective tire blows out, causing the car to flip and land on another car (with small children and several elderly passengers), killing them all instantly? Is that an "acceptable" level of error?

While you may not deal with such immediate life-or-death errors, you are likely dealing with issues that have eternal implications. What if you deliver a message that you threw together at the last minute that communicates something contrary to Biblical teaching and sends a listener down an ungodly path? What if your lack of ZDA causes you to condone a poor hiring process that results in an unqualified minister on your team who ends up abusing children? What if you turn people off to the message of the gospel because you failed to have sound financial practices?

A Zero Defects Attitude is vitally important regardless of the field and affects every area of personal and professional practice.

Zero Defects Attitude
Scriptural Basis & Devotional

I press on toward the goal to win the prize for which God has called me heavenward in Christ Jesus. All of us, then, who are mature should take such a view of things. And if on some point you think differently, that too God will make clear to you. Only let us live up to what we have already attained.

Philippians 3: 14-16 (NIV)

This foundational concept of Biblical "personal growth" (mentally, emotionally, and spiritually) as a follower of Christ has its own parallel metric in the professional life of a believer. Our desire to learn and grow both personally and professionally is an indicator of how much we understand about "what we have already attained" in Christ and whether or not we are preparing to become "salt and light" to the people who interact with us and observe our life at work.

Personal credibility is directly linked to the competence and maturity we display in the execution of our duties in the workplace. Whether our work is as a "leader" or as a "faithful servant" to others in authority, our grasp of the essential vocational elements of our profession sometimes projects just as clearly (or more so) to unbelievers that we are acting within a higher level of self-discipline and personal accountability than is the norm in the workplace.

Zero Defects Attitude
Self-Assessment

Using the scoring scale, rate each area of the question. At the end of the Assessment, tally the score by letter (i.e. tally the totals for A, for B, and C, separately).

On a scale of 1 to 5, where 1 is Never, 2 is Hardly Ever, 3 is Some of the Time, 4 is Most of the Time, and 5 is All of the Time,

1) How often is the constituent the focus of the work done by the organization as demonstrated by
    A. Each of the leaders in the organization?
    B. Each of the team members in your area?
    C. You?
2) How often is a sense of satisfaction about the work done by the organization (or pride of workmanship) demonstrated by
    A. Each of the leaders in the organization?
    B. Each of the team members in your area?
    C. You?
3) How often are promises kept by
    A. Each of the leaders in the organization?

B. Each of the team members in your area?
  C. You?

4) How often are errors, mistakes, and problems accepted as "okay" by
   A. Each of the leaders in the organization?
   B. Each of the team members in your area?
   C. You?

	Place your response for each question in the appropriate cell. Total the columns in the "T" row at the bottom.		
	Total of A — Leaders in the Organization	Total of B — Team Members in your Area	Total of C — You
1			
2			
3			
4			
T			

Zero Defects Attitude Reflection

ASSESSMENT
REVIEW & REFLECTION

Once you've completed each of the assessments, follow these steps:

1) Copy the totals lines for each area to the corresponding line in the table below.
2) Add each of the columns in the Totals row. Each cell has a maximum of 20 points so the Total amount should not exceed 160.
3) Calculate the percentage in the bottom row for each column by dividing the Total Amount by 160 and multiplying by 100.

	Leaders in the Organization	Team Members in your Area	You
Vocational Certainty			
Process Quality			
Administrative Consistency			
Executive Credibility			
Personal Authenticity			
Ethical Dependability			
KTP Culture			
Zero Defects Attitude			
Total			
%			

Reflection Questions

Now that you have scores calculated, reflect on them to understand how each group did. Consider each of the areas below as you reflect:

>Evaluate your Rankings. The first question to ask about the scores above is, are they a fair reflection of each group (leaders, team members, and you)? Were you too hard or too soft in your responses? Don't spend too much time considering this but make sure you weren't flippant in your responses or overly easy or hard on one particular group due to a personal bias.
>
>Evaluate the Differences. As you see the numbers in one place, how do the differences strike you? Are there differences between your score and the leaders or members of your team that stand out? If so, why do you think there are those differences? Is there a disconnect between your values and theirs?
>
>Evaluate the Deficiencies. Review each category for each group. Are there specific areas where any of them fell considerably short of the potential total? Why? How do you think they could improve?

Record your reflections below in the notes section.

Assessment Reflection

NEXT STEPS

Now that you've completed this Quality Management Devotional, there are opportunities to continue your personal and ministry development in the area of quality management through Progressus Education Services; and because you've completed this devotional, we'll discount the price.

Progressus (www.ProgressusEd.com) is an education-based service organization that helps organizations and individuals develop their quality management practices through training and consulting services. We offer a Certified Non-Profit Leader certification in partnership with the Quality Management Institute (QMI), with which we are an affiliate partner. The certification is offered with ministers in mind.

Through this training, you will be able to see:

- Excellent leadership of human resources leading to reduced staff turnover.
- Effective management of the budget and financial matters of your local church or ministry.
- Forward leaning structuring of church operational systems for more effective engagement of church and community.

- Stronger board and parishioner relationships that lead to more effective accomplishment of the mission and vision of your local church.
- Increased congregational participation and community involvement.
- Systematic practices for organizational leadership.
- Relating reasonably and competently to the business community members represented in your congregation with the personal and organizational capacity to offer them valuable, Biblically-consistent counseling and training. A spiritually motivated and financially successful business constituency within a congregation inevitably leads to a healthier financial basis for the mission.

This certification process will include an online, flipped classroom model that is self-paced. Additionally, there are discussion groups available with the leaders of QMI and Progressus that will help you think through the material as it relates to your personal and ministry practice. We will also coach you through a project that demonstrates your knowledge base of the QM principles. The cost of this certification program at the time of printing is $2,195 per person. Because you have completed this devotional, QMI and Progressus are offering a 15% discount on the course. That makes the course $1,866.

In addition to the certification training, Progressus goes a step further. We work with organizations to help them implement the quality management principles they've learned in the training into their ministries. We start with a quality systems review to assess your current status and where we can help the most. Then we help you implement the processes, procedures, and changes that will bring your organization growth through quality measures. Because we are mindful of ministry size and scope, we can work affordably with ministries of the smallest churches on up through large organizations.

For more information on our certification process or implementation services, please contact us through one of the methods below:

Telephone: (918) 895-1185
e-mail: jfischer@progressused.com

www.ingramcontent.com/pod-product-compliance
Lightning Source LLC
Chambersburg PA
CBHW021411290426
44108CB00010B/478